How To Gain

The Upper Hand

P.O.W.E.R. Tactics That

Get Leaders Results!!!

By:

Matt Episcopo

How To Gain The Upper Hand,
P.O.W.E.R. Tactics That Get Leaders Results!!!
Copyright © 2012 by Matt Episcopo Enterprises Inc.
Third Edition Copyright © 2017
ISBN - 978-0-578-17447-1

DISCLAIMER

www.MattEpiscopo.com   Office 877-525-1617

Printed in the United States of America

Dedication

There are a number of people I would like to thank who gave me their knowledge and insight through the years.

My friend and mentor Jim Chapman, who taught me the art of interview and interrogation and death investigation. Jim Foster, retired New York State Police (NYSP), who taught me NLP. Dr. Richard Ovens, retired NYSP, who taught me "Dress for Success". Al Joseph, retired Rochester PD, who taught me the art of building rapport and the investigative process. My partners while at the Madison County Sheriff's Office Joe Tallman and Mike Hayes; I would also like to thank Special Agent Mark Shelhamer, FBI; Kevin Costigan, DMORT; Mike Bailey and Sherman Jones retired Utica PD; Jim McCarthy and Joe Luker retired Oneida County Sheriff's Office; Chief Robert Young retired Cazenovia PD; Honorable Donald F. Cerio Jr.; all of the dedicated men and women of EMS, Fire Service, Law Enforcement and Military (Thank you for your service); Master Hidy Ochai; Eden Ari; Dariush Soudi and his amazing team; Dean Hankey; Joel Bauer; Ron Zollweg; Eric Henning; my brother Scott; sisters Payton, Diane and Denise; mother, Janet and father, Rocco; my friends and family.

I would especially like to thank my wife **Brenda** and son **Brandon**, who believe in me and have made this project possible. THANK YOU ALL!!!

Table of Contents

Introduction

"If there was one problem in business that you could solve that would have an immediate impact, what would that be, and why?" Following a presentation that I gave at a local Rotary meeting, one of the Rotarians pulled me aside and asked this excellent question. My answer is simple: communication, both verbally and non-verbally. My experience has taught me that communication is key to everything. This lesson has been proven over and over again, in my work in law enforcement, in my personal life and in my business dealings. Anyone in any kind of business relies on communication on a number of levels. Communication helps you understand the customer's need. It helps the customer understand what you can provide. It provides the framework, the foundation and the 'goods' to make the sale. Most importantly- good communication is crucial to having happy, loyal customers and a lucrative, successful business. Communication is also the hallmark of every successful relationship. Think about how much you talk and listen to people every single day. It's huge percentage of what you do.

In this book, I will prove to you that by learning some secret psychological tactics used by law enforcement, you can make an immediate impact on your personal and professional life. I call this my **POWER Persuasion System**. It will give you the "**Upper Hand**"!!!

I am privileged to have a wealth of distinguished professional experience that I can share with you saving you tens of thousands of dollars and years of training. I have trained thousands of police officers, business professionals and people just like you.

As I travel to different conferences I find everyone wants to know the secrets inside of law enforcement. Think about this, what is really popular on television today? Shows like NCIS, Bones, True TV, CSI, Criminal Minds and a variety of crime related documentaries are what people are tuning into. This shows people really have an interest in the law enforcement. I weave just enough of my 'tales from the street' to keep you on the edge of your seat.

One day I started thinking: if you did something wrong, you knew that you are going to get in trouble for it, and you knew that I was a police officer: why would you tell me? Can you think of any answers? If you thought, "If I tell this police officer what I did wrong I am going to be fired, maybe lose my house, go to jail, or pay big fines," why would you tell? Over the course of my 21 years, thousands of people did tell me about their crimes. My confession rate was the highest among my peers. Professionals often asked me if I was psychic. I find that you don't have to read minds when you have a communication system that works. This system is what I am sharing with you to make your personal and professional life soar.

My job as an investigator was to teach people how to tell the truth. I found that some people were scared. They didn't want to be scared, but they were afraid of what the consequences may be. My job was to help people overcome obstacles and to tell me the truth. How do I know it works for everyone? Because I didn't get to choose the people I talked to. I responded, ready for action, whenever the radio went off, or the phone rang and the dispatcher said, "Here is the call you have to go on...".

I didn't get to pick and chose a demographic of people I wanted to talk to. I used my POWER Persuasion System to get the upper hand time and time again, with people of every imaginable background. As a result, I am a firm believer that people are much more similar than difference might have you believe.

Of course you will find that you deal with people with a variety of backgrounds and cultural differences. My system teaches you simple and easy to use strategies to understand work through differences.

Another way that I know that my system works is because I have used the techniques that I am going to teach you in this book, and they have repeatedly held up under the toughest scrutiny in the courts. The players in the courts had all day to pick apart every single thing I did, said and my methods in order to win their case. And my methods held up under this intense scrutiny time and again.

I took these advance police strategies and converted them into an ethical business practice to give professionals like you tools you can use immediately and gain an edge that will skyrocket you above the others. You will have the upper hand!

A NOTE ON ETHICS:

The first thing that we need to talk about is ethics, because anything that is this good can be used for bad, as well. In this book, I am teaching you an ethical communication system, i.e. the 'good way of doing it'. Could you use it for bad? Yes, you could, but here is the difference: the end result will be very different. When you use the POWER Persuasion System to gain the upper hand the way that I am teaching you in this book (and in my workshops and lectures), the ethical way, you are going to have longstanding relationships with the people that are going to do business with you again, again, and again.

If you use these techniques unethically, you potentially may see short-term gain but then, the word gets out there and your reputation is ruined. My system is designed to build relationships for long-term success, not to provide the 'quick fix' for a quick sale. It's not worth immediate small gains to sacrifice long-term success and the ruin of your reputation.

So let me summarize. It's kind of like a cement block, for example. If you have a block, a block could be very useful as building a good foundation. When you put these blocks together you have a good foundation for what you're building. But if you take that block and clunk someone in the head with it, it's very bad. It might result in a short-term gain, but the long-term consequences do not result in your success.

MY BACKGROUND:

I was born and raised in central NY. In 1990 I was hired by the Madison County Sheriff's Office. For the first two years, I worked as a corrections officer in the jail, which housed local, state and federal prisoners. Prior to this, I had spent years as a volunteer fireman.

In 1992, I started the Madison County Sheriff's Office's First K9 Unit with my partner, a drug dog named K9 Cyclone. She was a pure bred Black Labrador Retriever, and she served until her retirement in 2000. She stayed with me until her passing in 2004, as the county's highest trained pet and beloved family member. I was a Patrol Deputy from 1993 to 1995.

From 1996 until 2001 I was a Criminal Investigator. From 2001- 2005 I quickly moved up the ranks to become the agency's first Sergeant of Investigations and first Lieutenant of Investigations. In 2005 I became the Captain of the Criminal and Civil Divisions.

In our agency that was the highest rank I could achieve without being elected or appointed. The Sheriff is an elected official and he appoints second in command, the Undersheriff. I reported directly to the Undersheriff.

I have been teaching interview and interrogation courses at various police academies since 2002. I also teach the process for death investigations. In addition, I teach leadership and management for officers coming up through the ranks as well as reporting writing. I have well more than 3,000 hours of specialized police training, some of which is by invitation only and most law enforcement professionals are not privy to.

I retired from the Madison County Sheriff's Office after more than 21 years of service as the most decorated law enforcement official in Madison County history. I have received a number of awards and citations, the highest of which is the Medal of Honor. Now I conduct training on my system and deliver presentations on related topics at conferences and workplaces and coach individuals around the country. I am considered to be an expert in communication, leadership and personal development. Oh, I perform comedy magic and became a certified Hypnotist as well!

I know you're thinking, "magic?" or "how can a cop be funny?". I became interested in and performed magic even prior to working at the sheriff's office. But for me, that really became my stress relief, and stress relief is critical for surviving 21 years in one of the most dangerous and stressful professions.

Every day I went to work with people that were generally not happy to see me (you know, drug dealers, rapists, child molesters and more). And so, comedy and magic helped me fill my need to see happy people. By performing comedy and magic, I make people smile and laugh- for me, the best possible stress relief. Today I have perfected a 'killer' show that plays to audiences of all sizes and ages. Over the years I have also enjoyed a distinguished 'career' in magic, but that's a story for another time.

SEGWAY

In this book, I am going to teach you my proven POWER Persuasion System to gain the upper hand in what I call 'block style'. My style of teaching is to teach you a block-by-block while building a solid foundation of understanding the system and the proper tools for success.

My POWER Persuasion system is made up of a variety of tools designed to give you the upper hand in virtually any situation. It is very important for you to have a big bag or a big box of tools because in every situation is different. The more tools that you have to pick from, the better it is going to work out for you.

I am also here to tell you that there is no 'best way' to apply each of these tools. There is a process with tools and techniques that work. From there, you will apply these tools in your own natural style.

Let's say that you think I am the greatest person in the world and you want to be exactly like me – well, you are not me. You are a unique individual. You can emulate some things that you like about me, but everyone is different and that's really cool. I encourage you to take the best from all of those people that you admire and respect, and put it into a package that works for you. Then, if you follow my system, you can't lose!

BREAK THE PARADIGM:

We all have our ways of doing things. My book will change your way of communicating, verbally and non-verbally, open your eyes to new ideas, and get you thinking. Training, like the information provided in this book, is one way to bring about change. My system is proven. If you follow along with it, practice and implement the system, you will be even more successful and I even think you are going to enjoy it.

We are talking total communication paradigm shift. So first of all, what is a paradigm? Usually, the accountants say, "20 cents", that's not what I mean. Here is a better example using monkeys that I use when I teach at the police academy:

First, start with a cage containing five monkeys. In the cage, hang a banana on a string and put a set of stairs under it. Before long, a monkey will go to the stairs and start to climb towards the banana. As soon as the monkey touches the stairs spray all of the monkeys with cold water. After a while, another monkey makes an attempt with the same result. All of the monkeys are sprayed with cold water. Pretty soon, when any monkey tries to climb the stairs the other monkeys will try to prevent it. Now, turn off the cold water. Remove one monkey from the cage and replace it with a new one. The new monkey sees the banana and wants to climb the stairs. To his horror all the other monkeys attack him. After another attempt and attack, he knows that if he tries to climb the stairs he will be assaulted.

Next remove another of the original five monkeys and replace it with another new one. The newcomer goes to the stairs and attacked. The previous new comer takes part in the punishment with great enthusiasm. Again, replace a third original monkey with a new one. The new one makes it to the stairs and is attacked as well. Two of

15

the four monkeys that attacked him have no idea why they are not permitted to climb the stairs or why they are participating in the attack of the newest monkey but they do it anyway. After replacing the fourth and the fifth original monkeys, all of the monkeys that had been sprayed with cold water have been replaced. Nevertheless, no monkey ever again approaches the stairs. Why? Because that's the way it's always been done around here.

Think about the above example and think about the places that you have worked in, where you work, whom you work with, and how things operate. Sometimes you are doing something and you don't know why but that's always the way it has been done around there. Training through my book or workshops is designed to break those paradigms and get you moving in a new direction.

Gaining The Upper Hand By Using The "POWER Persuasion" System:

The POWER Persuasion System is your new system to improve success in your life personally and professionally. I have taken my proven system and assigned an easy to remember moniker (POWER) with each letter representing a step in the process. How convenient! So if you can remember, "POWER" then you will remember the steps involved in using this process and gain the upper hand.

P- PREPARATION:

P stands for preparation. Preparation is critical to your success. It contains the first set of secrets from inside law enforcement. The POWER Persuasion System preparation phase includes confidence, leadership, dress for success, how to be your own best customer, tips to prepare and a powerful personal introduction sequence mixed with verbal and non-verbal secrets to give you the upper hand.

CONFIDENCE:

We are going to talk about confidence first, because confidence sets the tone for everything else. Everything that is going to follow is built up from a base of confidence.

I want you to think about your work, service or your product. Don't read on until you've though about your service, product or your business for a moment. Do you have confidence in your service, product or your business? I know this is a big statement to say but if you are not confident in what you are doing or selling, then you should not be doing this work or selling this service or product. Find yourself another line of work.

Confidence starts inside, and then allows you to portray that confidence externally. You are more confident internally if you know the outcome that you are facing. Let's just talk about basketball for example. If you have to take a free throw, and you picture yourself at the free throw line, you have the ball and you take a couple of bounces, and you make the shot. As a result, you actually make the shot. Studies have shown that people who practice mental rehearsal do better in achieving desired outcomes than those that do not. If you can picture yourself having a positive outcome you have a much better chance of achieving that outcome. In your mind you have experienced it already, and you have seen the fruits of your labor, and it is positive and it is happy, so you have confidence.

NOTE: there are a number of activities in this book. Please STOP and DO each of the activities for maximum benefit. You need to take ACTION! In my workshops and training seminars I am a very hands-on teacher. Your success depends on you to take action and complete each of the activities. Skipping them only short-changes yourself. You will see immediate results.

Activity: Confidence building

Stand tall, shoulders back, smile, make good eye contact when you walk past someone and say the following in your head; "I'm cool, I'm calm, I'm the best". Also walk through a group of people, NOT around them! Do it confidently and with pleasure. If some one is in your way say "Excuse me", NEVER "Sorry". What are you sorry for? Sorry is submissive. You are confident, you are a leader!

Now that you have your inward confidence, you have your outward confidence. You are going to play your inner game because your inner game is going to directly affect how you look and how you act. Once your inner game is winning, the way you look, act and carry yourself will exude the confidence you feel.

19

Later in this book, you are going to learn a great deal about interpreting non-verbal communication. It's not only important that you know how to read it but you have to know how to portray it to other people, because they are going to be sizing you up as well, especially within the first few seconds of meeting. When you meet someone for the first time, they are going to size you up quickly and assess the tone for your interactions with them moving forward. You must rehearse your inner game in your mind, and then you will see success, and when you see success you carry yourself confidently. This confident, optimistic tone is a great setting for a business interaction.

To boil this down, you trick your mind initially and then it becomes reality. This is one strategy I used to get confessions from people who have committed crimes, as well. When I was talking to somebody who had committed a crime, there were times when I did my homework and I knew what evidence I had. This allowed me to experience inner confidence and portray outward confidence, which set the tone for the interview. Merely by the way I carried myself (via confidence) an offender knew they weren't likely to get anything past me.

In criminal court you need one of three things to have a case. You need physical evidence, eyewitness testimony or a confession. The more that you have of the three, the better chance of a successful conviction. If I already knew I didn't need their confession did this give me confidence? Absolutely. Many times when I walked in the room and the suspect saw my confidence it became very intimidating. Often times they would think, "Wow! I better tell the truth because it is going to be better for me." And I worked hard to make sure that was the truth.

Activity: Mental Rehearsal

Find a quiet place, where you can be uninterrupted for 10 minutes. This activity can be longer and more detailed, or shorter if time requires. Picture yourself 'in the moment' of a big proposal or client meeting that you have yet to experience. One that you are nervously anticipating. Create a visual image in your mind of where this meeting will occur. What are you wearing? What are they wearing? Where are you? How do you feel? Now imagine yourself making the 'pitch', or presenting your product to the client. Imagine your delivery is complete and powerful. Practice it in your mind. Now imaging the client says, "yes" to your pitch. Imagine the deal is sealed. How do you feel now? Hold on to that feeling. Repeat if necessary.

You might be thinking that you're too tough to mentally rehearse your business. I hope not! If you are nervous or thinking this has a chance of not going well that will show in your outward confidence. Rehearsal is a tool that sets you ahead of the competition.

LEADERS AND PROFESSIONALS:

Sometimes the confidence that you portray makes people want to follow you as a leader.

In my career I have noticed there are people that are managers of situations and there are people that are leaders of situations. Simplistically speaking, a manager attempts to control details and situations. Leaders inspire, create situations and help others to grow. Tom Peters said it best, "Leaders don't create followers, they create more leaders". That is exactly what I did in my law enforcement career and what I do today.

Think about two or three people in your mind right now, who through your life you looked up to as a leader. Then I want you to take it one step further. Why that person? What it is about them that inspired your confidence in them? Why is it that you like that person and you have thought of them as a leader? What did you like about them? What drew you to them? What do they do that you could emulate in whatever profession it is that you do and help you make yourself a leader and instead of a manager? We will talk more about leadership and do an activity in the "R" section of this book.

Let's take a look at the word 'professional'. Name some people that you think are professionals. What profession are they in?

It is interesting to me that throughout most of the presentations that I do, the top two responses to that question are: doctors and lawyers. Why is that we as a group of people hold doctors and lawyers on such high regard? Why are they professional? Is it their education? Is it the amount of money that they make? Is it the trades and the service they provide to their community? What is it that makes us think of them as professionals?

I want you to remember my phrase, "People are people." When I meet someone genuinely everyone is on an even ground with me from the homeless person in the street to the CEO of a corporation or anything in between, everybody is equal in my eyes. Based on my personal interaction they go up or go down based on my experience with them.

The point that I want to make is after today, when you walk out the room, when someone asks; "Who is a professional?" the answer is you! You are all professionals or you wouldn't be reading this book. You have all been elevated in to the careers that you have chosen because people have trust and confidence in you and your abilities. Knowing that you are a professional, how do you walk the walk, as well as talk the talk? The next section will reveal a couple of secret techniques to gain the upper hand.

DRESS FOR SUCCESS:

Do you think how you dress matters? Yes, it does. Absolutely! I have taught this in the police academy for years to investigators and management, and I am going to teach this psychological secret weapon to you now. Do not underestimate the power of this. This will separate you from everyone else and set the tone for all that follows.

Many times I got called into work in the middle of the night. I always took five minutes to shave and put my suit and tie on and "dress to the nines". I can't tell you how many times when I showed up on the scene the press came to me because they thought I was in charge. I was dressed to impress and I was dressed for success. As you will see it makes a huge difference and will give you the upper hand!

I want to give credit where credit is due. Some of this information can be found in a publication from the National Criminal Justice Reference Service. They did a study and printed a report in 1979 titled *Jury Preconceptions And*

Their Effect On Expert Scientific Testimony. This was initially the basis for my teachings. Numerous recent studies by researchers and management companies confirm that the results still hold true. My twenty-one plus years of experience, research and a number of current articles back up what I teach now.

Upon first meeting within several seconds, approximately 53% of what you look like matters to somebody. Even more so today because we have become very "casual" in society. I am not saying that this is fair; I am just saying that's what the statistics say. People ask me, "Well, how do you dress?" And I reply, "Well, it depends on the situation".

First, you have to know what environment you are going to be in and what's appropriate for that environment. It may be appropriate to wear a Hawaiian shirt, Bermuda shorts, and flip-flops. It may be appropriate to have a tuxedo. It all depends on what situation you are in and what you are doing. You must do a little bit of homework, as there is no hard and fast rule. Clarify the expectations of the situation, and make an impression with confidence and appropriateness.

People ask me when they attend my workshops, "How should I dress"? My answer, "How do you want to be perceived"?

In a general business situation, the most appropriate dress is business professional. To gain the upper hand I am going to take it a step further for you. This particular information on dressing for success came from the above named study. Jury members were asked, "Who looked like a more credible expert witness?". From their responses about what makes a person appear more credible and my experience, I recommend the following:

Men appear most credible in a two-piece or three-piece suit (They tested almost the same). Black is by far the best!

For some reason, brown portrays distrust in people's minds, and orange is the most disliked color by both men and women. Therefore, avoid brown and orange.

The rule of thumb is also one patterned item with two plains. Don't go mixing stripes and checkers when you're trying to be a power persuader. A dark suit, a white shirt, and a silk conservative tie is most credible. Patterns should be mild, as wild patterns were not favored. For men it's black lace up shoes (polished), black socks, get a hair cut (short hair always fares best), no beards (unless you are interviewing for a job as a lumberjack!), mustaches are a possible negative, but if you must, make sure it is neat and trimmed, no rings other than a wedding ring or college ring, no earrings (if you normally wear one, take it out).

For women it is the business professional, "librarian-look". A woman appears most credible when she: is neat, has her hair tucked up, wears a knee-length black conservative **skirt suit** (no dresses), black shoes (no more than a 2" heel), wears conservative black hosiery (and no runs!), if she wears nail polish (not required), it is clear or a conservative color, minimal use of makeup (it should not be too noticeable), no more than one ring on each hand, one set of earrings only, glasses (if you have them) and briefcase. **Note:** A pantsuit is considered business casual, NOT business professional. Let's look at the numbers.

Appears A More Knowledgeable Expert:

Clothing type:
Suits 91% (2 or 3 piece for men, skirt suit for women)
Sports Jacket 3%
Other 6%
(Men ditch the sports coat !!!)

Color:
Black 100% best color for both men and women

Male dark blue suit 89%
Male dark brown sports coat 11%

Male with white shirt 80%
Male with yellow shirt 20%

Male with conservative tie 87%
Male with loud tie 13%

Female with skirted suit 78%
Female with skirt & sweater 22%

Female with hair up 69%
Female with hair down 31%

Female with gray skirted suit 64%
Male with dark brown suit 36%

Male with blue suit 73%

Female with gray skirted suit 27%

With glasses & briefcase 89%

Without glasses and briefcase 11%

Standing illustrating 89%

Sitting talking 11%

Let's talk about black. Studies show the color that inspires the most confidence in both men and women is black. Black is the ultimate power color. Think about it, who wears black in our society? Powerful people like judges, religious and political officials to name a few. These are leaders in our society.   Black is associated with power, elegance, formality, and mystery. Black denotes strength and authority.

Another reason to wear black is that it hides your body well. To your eye, anything blacked out is not important to look at. The only thing to look at is now your face and hands (and you will have a confident smile and good eye contact). People will focus on what you are saying. It allows you to focus on the conversation.

Here is my recommendation for the ultimate power suit. Go get a nice fitted black suit, black socks, black tie up shoes, white long sleeve dress shirt (if you want to kick it up a notch get a shirt with French cuffs and simple cufflinks. A nice dress watch. A simple silk tie, my preference is color on color, remember simple is best.

The color of your tie is directed by the mission at hand:

Red quickly attracts the eye and often is used as a symbol of authority and determination. Seen on business professionals throughout the world, red is considered a conservative color that makes for a "power tie." It is good to wear when fundraising.

Blue is considered a color of depth, trust and confidence. Electric blue is seen as a symbol of seriousness and knowledge, and is often used on conservative "power ties" with red. It is good to use when you need to effectively communicate your message.

Pink may not be very far outside the red family, pink ties appear positive, soft, compassionate and friendly.

Yellow is seen as cheerful and happy, gold tones give the perception of prestige and wisdom. It is highly visible so wear it when you want to stand out, good for networking and marketing.

White tests well and is a color that is clean, organized, shows simplicity and balance like Ying and Yang.

Women should wear a black **skirt suit** (as described above), a white blouse, or use the colors above for your blouse color depending on your mission.

Study shows the following to be a negative impression for females:

Dangling jewelry 99%

Big shoulder pads 97%

Low neck lines 95%

Bare legs 94%

Sport shoes 91%

Short skirt 60%

Study shows the following to be a negative impression for males:

No tie 52%

No jacket 50%

Polo shirt 66%

Jeans 82%

T-shirts 88%

Leather jackets 70%

Now remember, these recommendations are based on research and experience of what makes you look like the more credible expert, not on my personal beliefs.

I am not here to debate your style or beliefs, I am here to give you information that is proven to work and give you a huge advantage and the upper hand if you take action. It should also be noted that the researchers were "surprised by the strong positive reaction to their change in attire. Interesting, also, was the nature of the comments received".

Appearing credible and being perceived as an expert in your field affords you a huge advantage, giving you the upper hand. My students now refer to this look as "my uniform". It is the uniform of success! People value a credible person. Remember, people are sizing you up in the first seven seconds that you meet, and they are getting an impression of you. When you come in confident, with a smile and good eye contact, dressed for success, appearing most credible, looking like an expert with your briefcase, your power suit, and your glasses on, the response in the person's mind will be, "Wow!" I can't tell you the number of times I have had the door opened for me, received upgrades and discounts, got confessions and closed deals. IT WORKS !!!

ACTIVITY: Dress For Success

You will spend about $400, but that will turn into a lot more depending if you take action. Buy a new black power suit and accessories. Dress this way for 30 days and take notes each day of how different you feel, how you are treated, the compliments you receive and how it affects your business. Be confident and have fun.

Commanding respect is important, too. Some people have command presence and other people don't. Command presence is all about how you carry yourself. Think about how different you feel when you "dress up". Now you must match that with confidence. Dressing for success is absolutely important but just know what environment you are going in, dress appropriately and professionally for that environment, and it sets the stage for the interaction to come. Remember, "I'm cool, I'm calm, I'm the best", it will give you the upper hand.

BE YOUR OWN BEST CUSTOMER:

If you love your product or service so much, you better be using it! Be your own best customer and you'll lead by example.

There's nothing that I love more than when I get that phone call and someone (obviously not trained by me) is trying to sell me something. Recently, a guy called me on the phone, and he wants me to buy insurance.

I said, "I have one question for you," and I asked, "Do you have this insurance?" He was silent and I further asked, "If you don't have this why should I have it?" Think about that. I talked to him and convinced him to pass me up to the manager so I could train their sales team.

If he is not his own best customer, if he doesn't have this insurance, and he doesn't believe in it, he can't rave about it, and he is not excited about it, why should I be?

Do you actively use and advocate for your product or service even when you are not "at work"? People notice, and if are not using it in your personal life why should they? On the other hand if you are, and you are successful, people will be magnetically attracted to you and want to use your product or service.

Now think about what jobs you do, and be the best at it. That doesn't mean that you are better than every single person, but you have to believe in what you are doing and be excited about it.

In order to show your confidence and excitement, you have to be prepared. There are many different ways that you can prepare yourself. Regardless of what the scenario is, there is always some preparation that's necessary to set the stage for success.

PREPARE:

During my workshops in which I teach interview and interrogation at the police academy, the young cadets often ask, "When do we get to the questions list? We want to get to the questions to ask. We have that bad guy sitting right there in front of us and we need to know what are we going to ask?"

I tell them, just like I am telling you, if you follow this system step by step, by the time it comes to asking the tough questions (or in your case "closing") it will be very obvious. That is the easy part. All the build up to and steps you must take make it the easy part cannot be skipped, or it will not be easy. That is where I saw so many officers have trouble, and now I see so many businesses doing the same thing. Not having a proven system in place and taking short cuts, failing in the end, wondering why and blaming someone or something else on their failure.

We are going to get to those active communication strategies. However, there is a whole bunch of stuff that we need to do before we start to talk to that person. The same is true for you in your business. Think about it, if we start talking to someone and we have no background information or anything to go on, it can go bad quickly. Your opportunity is lost and we cannot afford for that to happen, so you have to be prepared, beyond reviewing the typical customer history.

First, and simple- have you looked them up online? Have you ever looked yourself up online? That is a good thing to do, because it is good to know what information is out there in cyberspace that people can access about you. Type your name or your customer's name into a few popular search engines and see what you find. You never know, they just might be searching you too! What will they see? Is it something you can use to your advantage? If so- point them to it.

If you are going to hire me for training or keynote speech, the first thing I will say is, "search my name on the internet. You don't have to listen to me, you don't have to listen to my sales speech, and you can do your own homework." There is nothing better than when someone fills in the blanks on their own- making that a very, very powerful tool. Check on social media sites and you might be surprised by what you see. All the information is going to give you some good preparation for your meeting.

It is going to paint a picture for you initially. A second strategy is to ask around about your prospect. If you have to meet with someone, just ask around your office or your network, "Hey, I am going to talk with someone, so what can you tell me about them?" That will give you a little bit of an inside scoop. That's the stuff that you are probably not going to find on the Internet or in files. You are just gathering as much information as you can so that you are little bit better prepared.

Now, think about the best time and place.

Let's say you have an office. You want to meet with this person, your office is a disaster. Maybe your office isn't the best place to meet with somebody. You might want to a conference room or go to a different site that is a neutral site. Consider likelihood of interruptions. Maybe a public place isn't a good spot, but just think about it.

This is a part of playing that game up in your head. "I need to talk with someone. Here is where I should meet with them. Here is a good time to meet with people." You know, if you are saying, "I have to meet this person at 11 o'clock at night in a private place," that offer just doesn't sound good, does it? It really doesn't, so think about things. Your intent could be perfectly fine because you meant no harm by it but someone on the outside wonders, "What were you thinking?" Preparation will eliminate a great deal of these mistakes.

INTRODUCTION SEQUENCE:

Now that you've imagined yourself achieving success, you've mentally rehearsed, you've prepared, and you're dressed for success, what's the next step for portraying confidence? Your greeting. The way you shake hands and exchange names is the next **Secret Upper Hand Tactic** for literally gaining the upper hand.

Simply put, good eye contact and a firm, confident handshake sets the tone that you are in control of this situation. Preparation will tell you those rare times when you are dealing with a person whose culture does not condone direct eye contact or handshakes. If you've prepared, you'll know this in advance. The majority of the dealings you will have with others will benefit from eye contact and good handshake.

Always take advantage of shaking someone's hand, for a few reasons. Number one, it's going to set up the tone for your interaction. Number two, it's going to help build rapport, a bonding experience with another. Number three, it is going to establish trust. There are many ancient theories regarding why someone extends their hand. Sometimes this could be known as your gun hand, so I am extending my hands so you can see that I don't have a weapon. The historical purpose is that a sign of trust is shaking somebody's hand. Number four, you can size someone up by the feel of the handshake. Was it hard, clammy, limp, held back, dominating?

Who has ever experienced the kind of handshake where the other person grabs your hand and flips it over, or where they come in for the shake with their palm flat down, forcing you into a subservient position for the shake? In my field, I find attorneys do that more so than anyone else. No offense to attorneys if you are a lawyer. I find that a dominant personality will instigate the 'over the top' shake. Even if this happens to you, always remember that you are a professional.

You are a leader. The whole idea that you want to portray is, "we are going to talk." You are setting the stage as if to say with your introduction, handshake and the utmost politeness, "I am the leader and you are the follower." So how do you win this handshake? You don't want things to start getting awkward. You're not going to thumb wrestle or twist their arm into submission. That it is just weird, right?

What's socially acceptable is quick touches by your free hand anywhere on the person from the wrist to the elbow while you say, "Nice to meet you," and that's it. A quick touch, done and that's it. When their hand comes over the top, or they twist you under, you keep your smile and quickly touch their arm with your free hand while saying, "nice to meet you", let go and it's over. You win. No big fuss.

But what happens if they shake your hand and touch your hand, arm or elbow at the same time? You simply touch their shoulder as you shake hands. Now you have just "one upp-ed" them. See how easy this is once you know the secret (The upper hand)?

The next *Secret Upper Hand Tactic* involves the exchange of names. Consider this exchange:

Matt Episcopo: "Hi, I'm Matt, What do your friends call you"?

Male Speaker: "Rich"

Matt Episcopo: "Great Rich, have a seat right over here".

Secret Upper Hand Tactic: What did I just establish? We are friends. His name is Richard, his friends call him Rich, I call him Rich, therefore I am a friend. All subliminal, of course.

You also want to know someone's name, as they preferred to be called, because you are going to continue to use their name. Use of someone's name is a rapport building technique. The last thing you want to do is call Rich by the name Richard, if that's what his mother called him whenever he was in trouble.

Secret Upper Hand Tactic: Boosting status through title. Depending on the situation, you may find it beneficial to boost your customer's confidence or to establish yourself as leader through the use of title. Do not use this secret carelessly. Be sure it is socially acceptable to use in the situation you are using it in. If you wish to build your customer up, use a title. For example, "Mr. Smith, my

41

name is Matt". Conversely, when you say, "Bob, my name is Mr. Episcopo" I gave myself a status and take his down a little bit. It all depends on the situation. You are giving titles more appropriately to even the playing field, that's all.

I am the leader, you are the follower. Now, the next technique that I use, which I plan to teach to you, involves giving a series of polite instructions for the customer to follow. If this doesn't feel natural to you- don't use it. It works with both men and women. You perform this with good intention (remember our ethics discussion above). It is considered socially polite, if you are my guest, that I offer you a chair. So I am going to offer you a chair and say, "Have a seat please. Just pull this chair right up to the table and make yourself comfortable".

Here is what I have done. First, I have been polite. Psychologically, again, I am subliminally telling my customer, "I am the leader and you are the follower". When I say, "Please have a seat. Sit down on the chair and pull it up to the table," that's at least three things I told him to do. He has done them and followed my commands. Note: when I pull the chair out to offer them a seat, I pull it out just a squeak further than normal. That way they have to follow my commands. They can't just sit in the chair at the table on their own without doing what I say. That is secretly planting little seeds for what's to come or setting the stage for successful communication, and tipping the scales in my favor.

To summarize, you have just learned a series of techniques for a successful, powerful, stage-setting first impression that is the first step in guaranteeing your success. It starts by mentally rehearsing your success and emanating confidence. Then by creating the most appropriate setting for your meeting, which you have prepared for beyond the typical client file review. A good handshake, with eye contact as appropriate is the first overt action with your customer. Utilizing secret tactics for building rapport and establishing confidence through the use of friendly names and titles. Finally, a polite sequence of commands to establish yourself as the leader while making your guest comfortable. You're off to a great start!

O- OBSERVE:

O is for observe. I'm going to teach you how to 'see' and observe before you learn how to 'talk'. The O phase, to me, is huge. Observation is related to a number of super secret tactics known by law enforcement. Dare I say, my mastery of the "O" phase is what leads so many peers to believe I am a mind reader. I'm sharing those secrets with you. You will not be a mind reader, but a powerful observer- even better. Study this, practice and master this observation section and you'll be reading so much more than the mind and gaining the upper hand!

Setting the stage for observation:

Upon initial interaction with someone, it is important for you to get a sense of what is the "norm" of the person you are interacting with. Setting the stage involves getting the person to interact in a casual, most normal way. During this stage, you should only be doing 15% - 20% of the talking. If you must talk, it should only be to ask an open-ended question so that you can listen.

An open-ended question is one that requires more than a one-word answer. I love this technique and I don't know why people don't use it more often.

Secret Upper Hand Tactic: to use with an open-ended question is to give a command in a way that sounds like a question in a very nice and polite way. We are raised to be polite, so we ask questions when we could use commands. I can ask a question or I could actually give a command that sounds like a question in a very polite and nice way. In my workshops this is one tactic that takes a little practice because it is not what we are use to doing. Once my students get this technique down, they are blown away by it! Ultimately, I am telling the person what to do, and when people are told what to do, I hate to say it, but people are likely to follow along and do it. If you tell them what to do, they will do it. As a result, they are following your lead. If you lead, they will follow.

Instead of asking someone a question, the super secret technique that I am going to teach you is not to ask the question, but tell him or her what to tell you. "Tell me..." That's your statement. "Tell me about your business?", "Tell me about your vacation?", "Tell me what you did today?", "Tell me what is on your mind." "Tell me what you are passionate about". When you say, "Tell me," the person feels more compelled to speak and you'll have some form of dialogue. If you ask a question beginning with, "Did you?" that is a yes or no question and they can just say, "No" and you are done, and that is the end of it. For example, "Did you have a good weekend?" could result in an answer of, "Yah", and your dialogue never begins.

You also learn very little about them. Instead, say, "Tell me about your weekend."

You're likely to receive a reply such as, "Well, I visited my mother, spent some family time, and took the dog to the lake to swim." As a result of the second effort, you have much more information to engage in dialogue about- to build rapport with them. You also have a greater chance to observe them acting 'normal' or 'norm them' while they are comfortable discussing something they know and like. Likewise, if the answer were negative, such as, "My dog passed away and my kids were sick", you'd have a chance to 'norm' that too.

Activity: Open Ended Question vs. Command Statement:

Phase 1: Engage someone in a 10-minute conversation and monitor yourself to talk only 15-20% of the time. When you talk, ask open-ended questions. Engage normally, and try not to 'force' the exercise.

Phase 2: Engage someone in a 10-minute conversation and monitor yourself to talk only 15-20% of the time. When you talk, give command statements to elicit dialogue. Use the phrase, "tell me....". Engage normally and try not to force the exercise.

Debrief the activity: How easy or difficult was it to talk only 15-20% of the time for you? What differences did you notice in yourself between using open-ended questions vs. command statement? What differences did you notice in your other person or in the types of responses you received? What parts of this technique are you most/least comfortable with? Practice!

Positioning and Questioning:

Observation is important to gather important information, A.K.A. ammunition. Information gathered can be positive information or negative information. You are going to be paying attention to what they say, how they say it, and their body language.

I want to make a statement about taking notes here. When you are talking with someone initially don't take notes at that point, because you haven't build rapport yet. If you start taking notes right away, people will get more concerned about what you are writing down, and why those things are important. This could really turn people off, if you haven't established credibility and rapport. It was really interesting training police officers, as they are so ingrained in getting information for their forms and reports. Through my workshops, they realized how much more quantity and quality information they can get when using my POWER Persuasion System to gain the upper hand.

I found, often that when an officer was engaging with someone they will ask, "What's your name?" "What's your date of birth?" "What's your address?" "What's this and what's that?" It feels like they are filling out their report right then and there. I'd always tell them, "Put that notepad away, right now". Build some rapport with people and you'll get more and better information. Later, it's appropriate to take some notes for the file. By this time, you have built a relationship with them, and they're expecting you to take notes.

A good lead in, is to say, "Wow, that is a lot of great information. Let me write a few things down to be sure I have it correct and understand what you are saying". By doing this you are installing confidence, reflecting the information to make sure you have accurate information. By taking "participatory notes", with their engagement, you will gain additional information. That is really what we want, more information and accurate information. Give it a try, you will be pleasantly surprised by how much better this style is and how much more successful you will be.

Here are little secrets to pay attention to in regards to setting the stage. Pay attention to what messages your own body language is portraying, as well as the person you are speaking with. The first is to notice the location of the clock in the room and seat the other person into position where they cannot see the clock. Once you start talking to someone, if they can see the clock, they are going to look at it, and then they are going to think of a reason why they have to be somewhere else other than here with you.

These little psychological things make a big difference. Also, notice the location of the door. If you can seat them closer to the door, where they can't see the clock, they feel like they can leave anytime they want to. You do not trap them in the room. Psychologically, that makes a big difference to people if they feel can run, they won't want to but they know that they can, so that is important.

Along with the clock, don't be looking at your watch. I had a job interview one time. The guy sat me down and he said, "Okay. Let's go through some stuff here," and he looked at his watch. Then he asked me, "What do you know about the company?" and he looked at his watch again. "Why do you want to work here?" He looked at his watch again. I said to myself, "I don't have the job-they have already picked the person." I asked him, "You already picked the person for this job, and my interview is just a formality isn't it?" He could not believe that I picked up on this within minutes of our introduction and admitted I was right. He confessed that before the interview he decided that he would ask me a few questions out of courtesy to make it look like a legitimate interview.

If your body language makes you look like you have to be somewhere else, that does not make the other person, your customer, feel like they are being listened to.

If you legitimately have to be somewhere at a certain time, tell the person upfront.

There is nothing wrong with being honest and saying, "Well, okay. Right now, it's 1:30 I just want to let you know that at 2:00 I have to go. I want to listen what you have to say right now. I'm just telling you upfront". They know it right upfront so there is nothing wrong with that. Likewise, it's a good idea to clarify the other person's time constraint right up front. This way, when they start to look at their watch (which hopefully they won't), you will know if they have a time constraint or if they want out of the conversation. If the latter is true, you may not be speaking to their genuine interest, or you may be speaking too much. Go back to listening and building rapport, then find common interest before you move ahead.

Secret Upper Hand Tactic: Give them a pen that is hard to open and observe how they respond. It is very telling, you will be surprised. Make mental notes and have another pen handy to give them in place of the hard to open pen if necessary.

MEN VS WOMEN:

Let's talk about men versus women for a minute because the differences are important to know. Now, this book is not the place for me to debate the six genders, the changing times and everything else related to diversity and stereotyping. Remember what I said in the beginning, "People are People. Period". However, there is research that illustrates some generalities in regards to brain processing of communication that differ between males and females.

My 21 years of experience with victims, perpetrators, witnesses and people on the street have proven these differences time and again. Always remember to understand what is normal behavior for the person you are talking with, and keep that in context when you explore these differences.

For example, a wife says is, "**Go** to the store. **Lay down** the mulch, wash **and** wax the car, and **get** the kids at school. Rent **some** videos and finish the **rest** of the dishes." What the husband hears is, "Go lay down and get some rest." It's OK to giggle while you read- that's funny (it's a joke)! But this section on differences in communication between men and women is no joke.

We are going to communicate with all kinds of people. All people are people but there are some differences.

One of the big differences is in how we communicate with people. It is good keep this awareness, if you are a man who is talking a woman or if you are a woman that is talking to a man. There are differences in communicating man to man versus man to woman, versus woman to woman.

Science tells us that men, in their brain, are right side dominant whereas women use both sides of their brain. The fact of the matter is men, if we go back to our cavemen days, have not really changed that much. Back in the cavemen days men were hunters, they were providers, and they were task-oriented whereas women were gatherers. Women gathered fruits and herbs in social groups. These behaviors were necessary for survival, and greatly influenced our genetics.

This resulted in a big difference that we see today: *men listen to respond, and women listen to understand.* If you know this, you are miles ahead in your next conversation with someone.

Let me give you some examples. Men, will listen until they think they have an answer, then their brains will go "Click!" and they are off line, and that's it. As soon as you start talking to a guy, with his task-oriented mind, this process is underway. While you are saying, "You know, geez, my car was down in the parking lot and someone hit my car..." he thinks he has an answer. You can try to keep talking but his is going to interrupt you and tell you what the solution is. That's what we guys do. Problem solved.

Whereas, with women, if you're talking to a woman and you tell her the same story, she is going to say, "Oh my! Keep going... and then what happened?" Women are good listeners. She will want to know whom it was, how it felt, if you're OK, what's next and so on. The woman will not feel compelled to suggest a final solution quickly, like the man does.

Again, back in the cavemen days, men went out on their own with a spear to find something to kill, kill it, and bring it back so everyone can eat: task oriented.

Women went out in groups and gathered berries, fruits, etc., and they would talk to each other, and listen. Big differences exist in how we communicate with each other and you have to know that going into any conversation.

Here's an interesting fact about this. In law enforcement we're concerned with deception and truth. This example relates to that. Everybody has what's called a 50-50 chance of detecting deception. There was a study conducted with every kind of group, nurses, doctors, lawyers, policemen, firemen, teachers and so on. Each group was given different scenarios and told by the researchers, "We want you tell us if someone is lying or not lying". There was only one group out of everyone tested that did any better than this 50-50 chance: the secret service. Now that you know that, think about it. In presidential protection detail, what is the secret service's job?

Observing. They are scanning the crowd to look at any body language that looks like it could be a threat to the president and they will take action on it. They are trained observers. They are trained better than the average person, and they are the only people that did any better in this study. Can you do that too? Absolutely, you can but it takes practice, practice, and when you are done practice, practice, and practice some more. Way back in the 'old days' there was a show on TV called, "The People's Court with Judge Wapner". I used to videotape (remember video tape?) the People's Court, watch it with the sound off, and I would try to figure out what was going on. What does this person say? What are they feeling? What are they doing?

What's the outcome of this case? And then I would rewind the tape and watch it with the sound on.

When you do that a few times, you will start really getting good at picking up clues and reading people's body language.

Activity: Observation

Try it! Find a court-TV type of show of something "Real". Watch it with the sound off. Try to guess what is going on. Then watch it with the sound on and see how close you were. Try this repeatedly.

People honestly believe I am a psychic. They really do believe that I have psychic abilities and I am not a psychic. I simply pay close attention to all kinds of things. When I go into a business, I can scan really quickly. I can tell if there is tension in the room, if there is trouble, is everything good, is it feeling okay?

Why should we care? Why should we care about non-verbal communication?

I'll tell you why we should care. 55% of human communication is body language, 38% tone of voice and only 7% are words. We all focus on the 7% words and miss the big picture. We don't think about, "I need to interpret non-verbal communication".

Very few professions, for example, police officers, specifically pay attention to that but it's unlikely you've spent considerable time training for this in your job.

I am going to challenge you today to just try a couple of these techniques I have taught you and watch the returns coming around, around, and around. It is going to be amazing for you. If you want more, attend my live workshops and we'll dig right into this in real time.

MODALITIES:

Think about modalities like family talk radio channel A, B, and C. (remember walkie-talkies?). If I am on A, and you are on B, and I say, "Can you hear me? Can you hear me? You are not hearing me are you?". What's important to know is that all people have three different channels or modalities that they communicate on. There's visual, auditory, and kinesthetic. When you are talking to somebody it is important to know what channel they are communicating on so you can tune in to that channel and communicate with them.

I list them in this order for a very, very specific reason, which you are about to see. The first channel is visual. Now statistically, men tend to be default set on visual. Women are a combination of all three.

There is not an automatic default for women but if you had to push the envelope and force a label onto it, then it would probably be defaulted on kinesthetic. But it is not always true so take it for what it is.

Visual people use words like, "I see...", "That's not clear to me.", "Looks good."

If the person you are talking to is talking in visual terms, you talk to him/her in visual terms. Visual people's body language shows that their heads are held higher, they breathe quicker and higher up in the chest, and everything is 'up'. The visual cue is an upward direction. We'll come back to this in a moment.

Let's talk about auditory communicators. They use words like, "I hear you," "That sounds good," "That's music to my ears". Their head is to the side and breathing is rhythmic with auditory people.

And the last is kinesthetic which is feelings or emotions. Kinesthetic communicators use words like, "That doesn't feel right. My gut says...", "that feels about right". Their body language leans toward the low direction. Their eyes move down, their heads bob down, everything is lower. This is why I listed the channels high, middle and low (visual, auditory, kinesthetic). You are about to see that with their linguistic program, which we are just about to go into, how true that is. So who has mastered this art of knowing what channel somebody is on?

Used car salesmen for example.

When you are going to look at a car the salesman will ask, "What is it about this car you like?" and they are listening carefully for your answer (Note: I would say "Tell me what you like about the car"). If you say, "Wow! The candy apple red paint and it's rims are really shiny", what channel of person are you? A visual person. If you say, "Wow! Do you hear the engine? The engine really roars and it's got a surround sound system" you are an auditory person. If you say, "It really hugs the road and I love the way it feels when I drive it" you are a kinesthetic person. Used car salesmen are masters at tuning in to your channel of communication and they usually know how to communicate on your channel.

NEURO-LINGUISTIC PROGRAMMING (NLP):

NLP, Neuro-linguistic programming is one of my favorite things. I am teaching this to you for your increased success and give you the upper hand. Do not use this at home. I am not responsible for divorces and fights. Here's what happens every single class that I teach this in, the participants go home and try it out because it is so cool. And they start asking questions and end up saying, "Darn... I didn't want to know that." Don't ever ask a question that you don't want to know the answer to.

I am not responsible for your use of this technique and remember this is an ethical persuasion process.

The body has two nervous systems, the central nervous system and the autonomic nervous system. The central nervous system, we can consider that as concerning itself with the physical and sensory functions that occur at a threshold of awareness. In other words, we have control over this. If I was to ask you to pick up your pen, your brain flares off the proper electric impulses, your muscles expand and contract and you pick up your pen: you can control that.

Now, there is also the autonomic nervous system. That's the division of the nervous system that controls bodily functions that appear to occur automatically without conscious thought of the body. This is the system that investigators target, the autonomic nervous system. I could ask you to not breathe and you could hold your breath and maybe you would pass out. If you passed out what starts happening automatically? You will start breathing again. Okay, even though you might be unconscious your body says, "I need to breathe," and it makes those things happen. It is something you do not have control over.

In your brain there is information and you have to consciously access that information in order to respond to questions. Your eyes are the clue as to where you are getting that information from and that's all this is. Is this the hard fast truth? It is not, but it is something to pay attention to, it is something that is interesting and it is something that will lead you down your communication path to ask better questions.

There is a lot of controversy about NLP, how to use it and its meaning. I am teaching you how I used it, and how I successfully used and taught it in law enforcement so you can do the same. This is the secret that most politicians don't want you to know. It could make or break an election.

To explain NLP, also called Neuro-linguistic eye movements, I've included a chart. The chart here is a face, as it would look if you were looking at somebody. We are going to learn which direction the eyes move, while retrieving or constructing different types of information.

If you draw a line down the middle of the face, it divides the face into sides. The right-hand side refers to your right, which is actually his left side, but I don't want to confuse you. When we refer to this as the right side, it refers to your right. Right side is for recall. Left side is construction. It is important to know if someone is recalling information or constructing information. (SEE CHART)

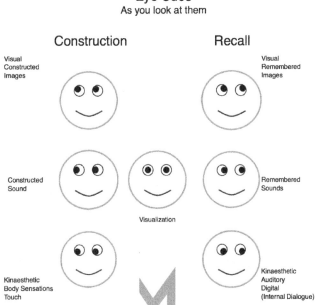

Eye Cues
As you look at them

62

Recalling refers to remembering information. Construction refers to constructing, or making information up. It doesn't mean the difference between truth and lie. It could, but it does not mean that automatically.

There is no lie detector or technique in the world that says this is truth and this lie. Truth vs. lie is determined by all the information put together based on corroboration.

For communication purposes, eye movements are going to tell you the channel that someone is communicating on, and whether they are recalling or constructing information. I'll tell you how, in just a moment.

NLP is good information to know, as it will propel you to new heights in your own information gathering. In any business you are in, information is power and key to your success. You can, prior to talking to somebody, construct questions designed to elicit a certain of response and if you don't see the response that you expect to see, you can say, "Why?" We don't say it's a lie, we say, "Why are they answering this way?"

This prompts you to inquire further, a process through which you will gather incredible information.

Eye movements will also tell you if you properly formulated your question because if you didn't ask a good question they will search around for the answer. Their eyes could move to the area of constructing information and the problem could be your unclear question, so keep that in mind as well.

As stated above, the order of visual, auditory and kinesthetic was introduced in order of up, even and down (high, middle, low). This is the way the eyes move when accessing related information. The side will tell whether they are recalling or construction.

First, you start by 'norming' someone's eye movements, as we discussed in the rapport building section. Noticing what eye movements are normal to the person you are speaking to. Then you will move into a series of questions by which you can assess their eye movements and responses. This is really fun to use during election candidate debates and celebrity interviews on TV. It makes watching TV a lot more fun!

If you are asking somebody a question and their eyes go up to your right, they are visually recalling information, something that actually happened or they are trying to see it in their mind's eye. Visual recall= up to your right.

If their eyes look to your right at an even level, it is an auditory recall. They are may be playing back what somebody said to them and hearing it. Auditory recall= over to your right.

Eyes moving down and to your right is kinesthetic recall, which is feeling. It can also be internal dialogue that they are having in their mind. Kinesthetic recall= down to your right.

Eyes moving up and to your left is visual construction. They are creating information about what something would look like. Visual construction= up to your left.

Eyes moving even to your left is auditory construction. The person is constructing something to hear. Auditory construction= over to your left.

Movement of the eyes down to your left is kinesthetic construction. his deals with construction of feelings and emotions. Kinesthetic construction= down to your left.

No movement, or a 'dead on stare' may indicate a few things. They may be trying to control their eyes (it wont last). The information may be readily available to them; therefore they do not need to search their mind's database for the answers.

This technique works best when you and your subject are facing each other, eye-to-eye. If you are sitting next to each other and you are using this technique, your eyes are already positioned to the side and the assessment will not be as effective.

Activity: NLP Eye Movements:

Find a partner, sit eye to eye and ask him or her the series of questions below, watching their eye movements as they respond. Read the question to yourself. Look up at your partner and ask the question, while watching their eyes during their response. Do not read the question to them off of your paper and then look up- you will miss the movement of the eyes. Scramble the order of these questions to keep them on their toes.

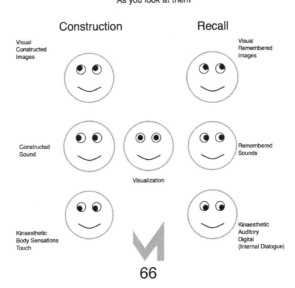

Eye Cues
As you look at them

Q. What was the color of the car you first learned to drive? You expect a visual recall response; eyes move up to your right.

Q. What would the offspring of a giraffe and elephant look like? As this does not exist, you expect a visual construction response, eyes move up to your left.

Q. Who is the first person to spoke to you this morning? Depends on what they said for what kind of response you are going to get here. If it were neutral, you would expect an auditory recall response; eyes move over to your right. However, it may elicit an emotional/ kinesthetic response, moving eyes down to your right.

Q. What would it feel like to sit in a tub of warm mud? You would expect to see a kinesthetic construction response; eyes move down to your left.

Make up a few of your own questions.

I'd like to share with you some notes on using this technique. Left-handed people sometimes have the opposite reaction than what you are going to expect. So if you are consistently seeing this construction response, you may ask, "Are you left-handed?" That is something that you might note during your observation. If they are writing something right-handed or left-handed that is something to make a note of. Don't give away your secret when they ask you how you knew!

Also, if someone's eyes are under construction mode you might simply clarify to ensure they understand the question- this way confusion is eliminated as the reason.

When you are talking to someone it is good to have proper eye contact in most cases, but don't stare because that's creepy.

No one likes to be stared at, so don't stare at people. Eye contact is something you do occasionally and casually.

When you notice a shift to construction response, remember to ask yourself, "Is it timely and consistent?" Spending a good amount of time in rapport building phase is important, because to have casual conversation with someone will allow you to see how the person interacts normally. When you shift from rapport building and start talking about your intended topic, does something change or is there a shift within the person you are taking? It's important to know why a shift occurred, if it did.

NON-VERBAL COMMUNICATION:

Nonverbal communication is my specialty and the crux of the POWER Persuasion System and gaining the upper hand. Let's go over some things that might be important for you to know, so that you'll understand why command knowledge of nonverbal communication gives you the upper hand. Statistics say that of all human communication, only 7% of the message received comes from what you actually say. Appearance, handshake, posture, smile, eye contact and nonverbal communication make up the most of our communication. No doubt, we want to master the 7% of what we're saying. However, we're going to spend our time on the remaining 93%.

Remember under confidence section, we discussed eye contact? Studies show that 67% of people surveyed reported that lack of eye contact was a negative. Lack of eye contact can break trust. Don't let that happen to you! Use eye contact to build rapport. It helps build trust and confidence. Use eye contact when shaking hands and maintain eye contact at least 60% of the time. You don't want to consistently stare at people.

You have to break eye contact once in a while, but a consistent lack of eye contact does not portray leadership or confidence.

Positive posture says a lot, as well. Your posture, sitting up straight, leaning in, smiling and nodding of the head are all signals that you are paying attention and are interested.

Open body is critical for you, and for them, when making any moves toward a sale. Crossed legs and folded arms are barriers. My experience comes from the interrogation room. You are not going to interrogate people, but will benefit from the tactic. When I am going for a confession it is a known fact that no one will ever confess when he or she is in a crossed position.

Also no one will make a purchase or say "yes" when in a crossed position. My job was always to unfold them, get their arms to uncross, and get a confession. With that being said, there's ways of doing that. I could physically take someone and unfold his or her arms- I wouldn't suggest that you do that. You can simply hand them a bottle of water. This is being nice and uncrossing them at the same time.

Another, highly recommended tactic that I used successfully was going back into rapport building. By giving the person space and going back to rapport building, they will uncross themselves. If someone is in a crossed position, they are either not either believing you or they feel threatened. You know, this is not a good thing. So take him or her back to the happy place and talk about what he or she likes. Build some rapport again and they are going to start to ease and unfold for you. You have to play that inner game again smile and be confident.

Studies show that 33% of people surveyed reported that bad posture negatively impacted communication and 21% said crossing arms over chest was a negative, so let's stop right there. Why do people do this? Back in our cavemen days you didn't have a chance to think about things. Your survival relied on things happening automatically within your body. When you fold your arms over your chest, you are inadvertently covering all of your internal organs-everything that is important. You are naturally protecting your internal organs. Of course this happens subliminally.

You are not saying out loud, "Matt Episcopo is threatening me, so I am going to protect my internal organs right now." It's a subliminal process that occurs instantly without thought.

Think about this, you are driving down the road minding your own business and a car comes out of a driveway and backs out right in front of you. What happens instantly?

Many things without you even thinking about it. You will begin to sweat a little bit and your heart rate goes up, the blood goes from your outer extremities into your internal organs. It all gathers and you might have that rush or tingle as the blood moves.

Why does this happen? Number one, your body sweats because again back to the cavemen days, if someone was going to grab you, your body provides a natural lubricant to slip away or deflect the glancing blow so it doesn't stick. The blood rushes away from your outer extremities so that if you are cut you don't bleed out and it goes to where it is needed to protect your internal organs. All of this happens in an adrenaline rush and it happens instantly. How long does it take to come off of that response? It could be a couple hours. It takes a while to get your body to calm back down to normal again or where it was before that happened. But it can go from zero to 100 in .5 seconds. So when these things happen, it creates stress within the body. Stress within the body causes people to do things that we observe.

Sometimes, when I was an investigator, I would look at someone I was interviewing and I would think, he looks like a one-man-track-meet-in-a-chair.

He is sitting in his chair clueless. He'll move the chair around, stretch a little bit, and fidget. What is happening? He is full of stress and the only way the body can dissipate stress is through movement, so he would move. And sometimes the blood rushing makes people's nose tingle. Your blood moving makes your capillaries tingle. As it all adds up, you'll see the person itching, twitching, stretching, sweating and start rocking. It's *really* easy to see once you know what to look for. You will laugh and say, "How did I miss that?"

The angle of your body indicates some very important things. It can indicate interest, leaning in as if they want to hear you. Some people, without knowing it, aim towards the door and they are saying non-verbally, "I cannot wait to get the heck out of here". So paying attention to these things tells you what they are thinking about.

Pointing your finger is another thing. Pointing at people is considered aggressive or rude, it is like scolding. Don't point at people, it is a negative gesture. To emphasize a point with your hands, try a technique called steepling. Steepling is touching your fingertips from each hand together while pointing to the sky. Usually, the higher up the more confident you are. Not so much that your palms touch- that is praying. When I would have to testify sometimes in court, I used steepling very effectively.

Communication around the table. Families communicate around the dinner table. Well, they used to. In a business situation, a table represents a barrier. You cannot always control this because you don't know where you are going to be. If I had my choice and I could control my environment, I would have a nice chair that had cushions and it could roll around and the other person would have a hard wooden chair. Only because I can roll around and move if I want to, but they can't, so it forces them to give me non-verbal communication cues.

Sometimes they will hook their feet around the bottom and that is another thing to notice. If I have a table between us, I am only seeing from their abdomen up, so I cannot tell what their hands or feet are doing. He could be sitting on his hands and I have seen people sit on their hands and lock their feet under the chair, attempting to hide their nonverbal cues.

A table, crossed arms and crossed legs are all barriers. When a person puts a barrier up in your interaction, keep your distance and keep good posture. We have already talked about positioning them by the door.

Sometimes you will see people talk with their hand over their mouth. Many times this is concerning to me because it is almost like they are trying to keep the truth in. When people talk through their hands, that is a red flag that you need to explore further.

WHAT IS BODY LANGUAGE?

Body language is the unspoken or non-verbal mode of communication that we do in every single aspect of our interaction with another person. It is like a mirror that tells us what the other person thinks and feels in response to our words or actions. Body language involves gestures, mannerisms, and other bodily signs.

Would you believe that in real life situations, 90% or more of the messages that we convey to other people are transmitted through body language and the actual verbal communication by words accounts for only 7% to 10%?

Our ability to use body language in a positive way and to read other people's minds through their body language separates the men from the boys (or women from girls), and can be a powerful tool to our overall personality development. Imagine creating a great impression for work, business, and love by being knowledgeable in this not-so-common yet powerful field of study. It is the unspoken tool to a successful life.

Reading the Signs:

We use body language everyday in our lives to get our message across, to achieve positive feedback in our lives, and to get whatever we want. We use this language all the time, but we may not be aware of it. Moreover, this language doesn't only involve the mouth but the whole body as well.

Could you even imagine the awesome power of applying it? With it, you'll be able to interpret other people's inner emotions even if they're not directly expressing it. You'll also be able to modify your behavior to fit the situation. You'll get them to like and trust you. What words cannot do, body language can.

In this chapter, we shall explore the various body gestures or movements conveyed by people in different scenarios. Let's begin.

Suggesting Interest:

It is important to know if people are interested in what you are saying; otherwise, you are just wasting your time.

Just imagine you are a science teacher. You have always been interested in science, so you assume that your students feel the same way as you do. But are they really interested? Are your teaching methods good enough to arouse their interest? Unless you can recognize the different body signals your students are conveying, you would never know how they are adapting to the subject matter. And unless you find out if staring continuously at you without blinking the eyes is a sign of interest or an indication of being in dreamland, you simply could not take the necessary steps to adjust to their learning needs.

Here are some of the movements exhibited by people who are interested in what you are saying:

• They maintain eye contact more than 60% of the time. The more wide- opened the eyes are, the more interested the person is. In fact, a person maintains eye contact more when listening than when talking.

• Their heads are inclined forward.

- They are nodding their heads. Such action means that they're agreeing with you. That means they're attentive and listening.

- Their feet are pointing towards you.

- They smile frequently. But take note, not all smiles convey the same feeling. An oblong smile is not genuine. It is used to show courtesy, but not necessarily happiness or friendliness. The lips are withheld completely back from the upper and lower teeth, forming the oblong shape. This is usually the smile that many people exhibit when they feign to enjoy a lame joke.

Indications That They're More Open to Agree with You:

When you were a young child, have you ever tried to decode what your parents' facial expressions mean when you ask them to buy you a new toy or to take you to Disneyland? A frown would likely be a "No!" But a nod would make you jump with joy. As you grow older, it has become a necessity to be able to detect if other people will agree with your decision or proposal. This is an ability that will truly help negotiators, employees, and even lovers to succeed in their ventures because they would be able to change their approach early enough to adjust to a specific situation.

There are certain hints to indicate if people are more receptive in accepting your ideas. Some of these are:

• Their hands are flat on the table.

• Their palms are open.

• If they're stroking their chin, they're thinking. They may agree with you after careful evaluation.

• Their heads are inclined forward.

• They are nodding their heads.

• Their legs are spaced out from each other.

• They smile frequently.

• They unbutton their jackets. This indicates friendliness and willingness to collaborate with you.

• Their hands are open. This also indicates genuineness.

• They place their hands in their chest. This signifies openness and conveys sincerity, honesty, or dedication.

However, a woman putting her hands on her breast is a defensive position and may indicate that she is surprised or astonished.

Indications That They are Thinking:

People think all the time. But different individuals make different body movements based on the type and intensity of their thinking. Some of their actions are written below:

• They're stroking their chin. This means they are assessing the advantages and disadvantages of the proposal/idea being presented.

• They take their glasses off, after which they may either (1) clean them, or (2) put the tip of the frame in their mouth. They are buying themselves some time to think things over. A frame in the mouth would also likely indicate that they need more details and they are willing to listen.

• They are pinching the bridge of the nose most likely with eyes closed. People doing this are engaged in very deep thought. They may be involved in a difficult situation, where they are aware of the consequences that may occur as a result of making crucial decisions.

- They put a palm below the chin, index finger pointed and extended along the cheek, while other fingers placed beneath the mouth. This gesture more likely indicates thoughts that are criticizing or antagonizing other people.

- They walk with the head down and hands behind the back. People who walk this way are probably worried about their problems, and they are thinking of ways to solve them.

Indications That They Are Frustrated/ Dismayed:

A basketball coach whose team loses by a point may say "Aaarrrrrrr!" or he may just keep quiet while making certain body movements that indicate how disappointed he is.

Here are some hints that indicate frustration.

- They are scratching/rubbing the hair or the back of the neck.

- You often hear the word "Tsk."

- They kick the dust or air.

Indications That They Are Action-Oriented:

People who are goal-oriented and highly motivated may not only be recognized by how they speak. Their actions actually speak louder.

• They walk at a fast rate while swinging their arms loosely.

• They put their hands on their hips, usually with legs apart.

• They walk with hands on their hips. This may indicate a spurt of vitality at the moment, but may be followed by sluggishness.

Indications That They Are Defensive/Hiding Something :

The mouth might keep a secret, but certain gestures could indicate that people are hiding something they don't want others to find out, such as:

• They walk with their hands in their pockets.

• They cross their arms.

• They hide their hands any way they can.

Indications Of Boredom:

Imagine your boss is doing a presentation and all employees are required to listen. You noticed that many of them are clicking their pen, tapping their feet, and drumming their fingers. After the meeting, you hear the boss ask them, "Did you enjoy the presentation?" They would say "Definitely!" But you know better. Their actions indicate just how bored they are. It feels good to know body language, doesn't it?

Some signals conveyed by people who are bored and disinterested include:

• Head supported by the palm, often accompanied by drooping eyes.

• They show inattentiveness by staring at a blank space (eyes not blinking) or by looking around frequently.

• They are pulling their ears. This may also signify that they want to interrupt while another person is talking.

• They are clicking a pen non-stop.

• They are tapping their hands or feet.

• They yawn incessantly.

- Their feet or other body parts are pointing to the exit, as if they are very eager to leave.

- They move restlessly in their seats. This could also mean that they are not cozy or at ease, or they might just be exhausted.

- They cross their legs and constantly kick their foot in a very slight motion (particularly done by females).

If you're the one making the presentation and you discerned that your audience are displaying signs of boredom, don't start talking faster or louder. Refrain from such act even if your instinct tells you to do so. Instead, say, "Hold on. I feel that I'm losing your attention. What's up?" Hear what they have to say. You may discover what's actually preventing them from keeping up with you.

Signals Conveying Excitement or Interest:

If you have experienced getting a promotion, receiving a special gift, or winning a contest, I bet you've done any of the acts made by excited people when you first discovered about your blessing. Some of the movements made by excited people include:

- They rub their palms against each other.

• They clap their hands.

• Their heads are tilted forward.

• They cross their fingers (usually comes with the hope that something big or special will happen).

Signals Exhibiting Confidence, Authority or Power:

People with a high degree of self-confidence are normally more likely to be successful than those who have low self-esteem. Moreover, those who exhibit authority or dominance usually come out on top because they subconsciously make other people feel weaker. So how do they move?

• They maintain firm eye contact and rarely look at other body parts underneath the nose.

• They speak with a low-pitched, slow-paced, downward-inflected voice.

• Chin tilted upwards.

• Chest projected outwards.

• They maintain an erect posture, whether standing or sitting.

• They sit in reverse, with the back of the chair serving as their support or shield. People who sit in this position are known to be bossy and aggressive.

• Their hands are clenched behind the back.

• Their hands are placed beside the hips.

• Their feet are on top of the table.

• They have a firm handshake, palms pointing downwards.

• They lean back with both hands supporting the head.

• They move with precision and with no hesitation.

• They walk solidly with forceful arm swings.

• They join the fingertips of both hands together (small finger of both hands joined together, ring finger of both hands joined together, and so on). Palms of both hands are not in contact with each other. The higher the hands are elevated, the more confident they are.

• They extend one leg over the arm of a chair they're sitting in. When they do this, it may also mean that they are apathetic, disinterested, or unconcerned. They may be exhibiting the "I don't care" attitude.

Moreover, you can declare your domination over other people by rising or elevating yourself from them. It is not unusual to see taller people being in control over the situation.

Choose a chair or location where other people will have to "look up" on you. They will subconsciously think they are weaker and can easily be manipulated.

Signals Of Anger/Resistance:

Many people rarely let their anger go out of control. They are more likely to restrain their raging emotions. You must therefore be able to recognize any gesture that signifies wrath or resistance to prevent any possible chances of the fireworks exploding. Here are some hints:

• Their fists are clenched.

• Their hands or feet are tapping.

• One hand is clutching the other hand, arm, or elbow.

• Their arms are crossed over the chest.

• Their eyes are blinking constantly.

• Collar pulled away from the neck, like letting some air in during a hot day in the summer.

• They kick the dust or air.

• Their arms are vertically placed on the table while the hands are gripping the edge. Beware when they do this because it might mean something like "You better get this done or else!" or "Better listen or you'll regret this!"

Signals Of Nervousness/Tension:

Nervousness can be a turn-off. If you're going to be interviewed in a television show (hey, who knows?), you should be aware of your body movements. Signals conveyed by nervous people include:

• Their fists are clenched.

• Their hands or feet are tapping.

• The bottom edges between the fingers of one hand are clenched with the bottom edges between the fingers of the other hand. This is the position of the hands when praying.

- Hands are interlocked (flesh between thumb and index finger of one hand joined with flesh between thumb and index finger of another hand) and pressing each other.

- They speak in a high-pitched, fast-paced, stuttering voice.

- They whistle to conceal and fight their nervousness.

- They are often clearing their throat.

- One hand is clutching the other hand, wrist, arm, or elbow.

- Their arms are at the back, where one hand is pressing the wrist or arm.

- Their arms are crossed, but they are gripping their biceps.

- Their legs are crossed while standing.

- They have a wilted handshake, palms pointing upwards.

- Their eyes evade you.

- Their ankles are locked or glued to each other. When accompanied by clenched fists, this may indicate that they are holding back strong emotions or feelings.

- They don't smoke. What?!? You thought people smoke because they're nervous. But it is in fact the opposite. People who smoke only do so when they are not tensed in any way.

When you hear them say "Whew," it means they are previously nervous but are now relieved because their problems have been solved or they have survived a big challenge.

Signals Made When They Are Doubting or Suspecting You:

It's sometimes difficult to assume whether you are being regarded as a trustworthy person, or you are being thought of as someone who is full of nonsense.

Here are some clues that may indicate suspicion:

- They glimpse sideways from the corner of one eye.

- They are rubbing or touching their eyes or ears.

- Their hands are tucked in their pockets.

- Their arms are crossed over the chest.

- Their glasses are dropped to the lower bridge of the nose, with eyes peering over them. This movement may indicate that you are being examined closely (to the point that you get self-conscious).

There's one act you usually do when you are the one doubting yourself - rubbing or touching your nose. This subconsciously occurs when you are uncertain of how to answer a critical question or when you are concerned of other people's reaction to your answer. Watch yourself!

Signals Made When They Need Reassurance:

Some people have this disorder where they feel that they are always making the wrong decisions. "Should I really buy this? Maybe I should wait for a sale." "Can I really get a better job after I resign from this company?" These people do certain actions to reassure themselves that they have made the right choice, that everything will be ok.

- They stick a pen in their mouth.

- They squeeze the chunky part of their hand.

- They rub the back of the chair (while sitting).

91

- They clamp their hands with thumbs touching against one another.

- They bite their nails (in some cases).

- They touch their throat (for women).

- They jiggle the coins in their pockets. (for those who are concerned about their riches).

Here's what certain types of people would do when they want to reassure others:

- A woman gives reassurance to another female by holding both of her hands and sometimes hugging her. The facial appearance of the consoling female matches the solemn mood of the other female.

- A politician who would like to reassure you that he will be doing a good job when elected in public office would shake your hand with his right hand and cup it with his left hand.

Indications of Pride:

• People often show how proud they are of their material possession (for example, a car) by leaning against it or by touching it. You can see the sparkle in their eyes and you can sense the thrill in their voice.

Indications of Deception:

How do you know when someone is lying?

People lie for a variety of reasons. It may be to cover up a fault or embarrassment, to avoid upsetting other people, to encourage when no hope can be perceived, or to be spared from petty hassles. It may also be due to more serious psychological problems such as delusional imaging or extreme vanity.

Here are some indications that are conveyed by people when lying:

• They speak in a high-pitched, fast-paced, stuttering voice.

• They are constantly swallowing and clearing their throat.

- They try their best to avoid having eye contact. This applies particularly to people who want to avoid discussing a certain topic.

- They look somewhere else and glimpse from the corner of their eye.

- They stick their tongue out to moist their lips.

- They are blinking rapidly.

- They rub their throat.

- Their arms are crossed over the chest.

- They are constantly touching parts of their face, especially the mouth, ear, and nose as if covering them.

- They scratch their head or the back of the neck.

- Their poses are closed, descending, and insecure.

- Their hands or feet are tapping.

- They always look down with shrugged shoulders.

- They are constantly moving from one place to another or changing their poses.

- They are projecting parts of their body (feet) to an escape route (door).

Don't Jump to Conclusions:

Every person has a unique body language. Although silence usually denotes that an individual is reserved and relaxed, sometimes it means information that was presented is sinking in, some people keep their anger within themselves and stay quiet. (This is very unhealthy because rage kept up inside can explode furiously anytime, causing serious casualties). A wide open mouth may indicate shock or astonishment for one person, while another person who performs this gesture could just be concentrating intently on a task he's doing. Constantly touching the mouth may indicate lying, although the real reason might just be that the mouth is itching.

One way to overcome this dilemma is to watch out for other signals that jive with the body language being exhibited. For example, you can confirm if a person is really nervous if he exhibits many of the qualities of nervousness described above. Judgment based on one or two gestures only may not be accurate enough, although they can be dependable. Be aware of the body language, but also combine your observations with the spoken words to get more hints regarding the inner feelings of another. Use this power to your advantage.

Activity: Observing Body Language

Observe the body language of another person. You could be sitting near them in a restaurant. It could be someone in a business meeting. Observe a friend during a conversation. Practice over and over again. Make a journal of what you noticed and the context for the observation. The best way to get good at this is to practice and illicit feedback to check your accuracy.

W- WIN THEM OVER:

Winning them over is the next phase, and here the secret tactics become.... Well, more tactical. This is what I formerly taught police officers in order to be successful, and it generally comes down to establishing, building and maintaining rapport.

Establishing, Building and Maintaining Rapport:

People like people like themselves. Re-read that sentence and think about that for a moment. People are comfortable and have a positive experience when the person they are interacting with feels familiar and understandable- like himself or herself. We've alluded to this several times above, and now we'll dig into it a bit deeper.

I cannot tell you how many times I have talked with somebody and said very little, "Uh-huh, keep going...", "... and I know what happened with this one..." and at the end of the conversation they will say to their friends, "That guy is great. I love him". That's the attitude they have because they really feel a sense of connection because I just allowed them to talk. When you let someone talk, they are going to talk about themselves. Because you are there, they positively associate you with their content of what they talked about.

We know people do business with people that they know, like, and trust. When I say, 'do business', think about the roles that you are in. It doesn't have to be that you are selling anything. But if you have a co-worker, or if you have a boss, or students, or whomever you are dealing with – if they don't know you, they don't like you, and they don't trust you, it is going to be a lot more difficult to do your job. In the past we bought from companies, whose brand we knew, liked and trusted.

Remember commercials talking about the 'trusted brand'? It is no longer that way. We now buy from people. People have a social media presence. Sometimes you can text them, sometimes you can interact with them on Facebook, Twitter, Skype or Zoom.

97

There are so many different ways of communicating with people and they build rapport with customers. You have to personally be the trusted brand.

Secret Upper Hand Tactic: for baseline rapport building: asking an open-ended question (or carefully formatted command statement) that elicits a multi-word response on a topic that is very, very positive for the speaker.

Activity: Rapport Building: *Talk to a colleague and ask him or her, "If you didn't have to be here today, you could do anything you want to do, and you had the choice of doing anything you want to do with no restrictions, tell me what you would chose to do?". Observe their body language. Notice the positive indicators.*

The next step is to find something that you have in common with something they like. Caution- you are looking for something common to discuss and build rapport. Be careful not to divulge too much personal information, as your safety and image could be jeopardized. Finding a safe common topic could be simple if you ask the above stated question and they answer with something you'd like to do too.

For example, if your colleague tells you he would like to spend the day golfing, and you like golf- you're in luck! You can ask what's the best course he ever played, etc. Always keep the follow up questions framed to illicit positive answers. If you ask how often does he play, you might bring out sadness that he doesn't play enough. Work hard to keep the conversation upbeat and positive.

However, if you don't know about golf, you don't want to pretend that you do because it will become obvious very quickly and your credibility will be shot. So what do you? One tactic is to be honest, admit that you don't know a lot about it and ask him to tell you more about it. Now he is the expert, and that elevates his confidence and positive associations. That's what you want during rapport building: you want people to feel good about themselves, and talk, and talk, and talk. And while they are talking, you are observing facial expressions, body language and eye movements. You are norming them.

In summary, if you know about the topic the person raises, run with it and you're building rapport. If you don't know about the topic, let them be the expert. That is a great way of building rapport. You want to make sure that when you are building rapport, you are building long terms business relationships. Building rapport is for the long haul. It is not just for talking to that person today, or right now or in the moment. So that means when the conversation is done, you want to check back in with them. Follow up is so important because not a lot of people do it. The feeling you leave them with and maintain is equally as important as the feeling you gave them in the moment.

You want to leave your customers, students, peers, bosses, etc. saying, "Oh, my goodness. That guy is great. I cannot wait to work with him again and he really knows what he is doing…".

You want people to get excited because once that person is excited they are going to tell their friends, they are going get excited, they are going to seek you out because you are the expert in what you do. This is how you get that ball rolling in a positive forward momentum. You are planting the seeds with rapport building. All along, you are watching your body language.

Another **Secret Upper Hand Tactic** of rapport building is commonly known, rarely used. Reflection to understand the speaker's intent is very important. It's good to listen to what they are saying but you want to make sure that you are clarifying that message also. Start out with a phrase like, "So if I understand what you are saying …" and summarize in your own words the intent of the message the speaker just said. This gives the speaker a chance to hear the message and if it is not correct, they will correct you.

A powerful super **Secret Upper Hand Tactic** for rapport building is to take your customer on a journey. How many people do you meet with on a regular basis? Do you use your office as the meeting place? We are talking about building relationships long-term. So imagine if you said to them, "Let's go to a local coffee shop this time." The next time, "let's meet at a restaurant." The next time, "let's meet at my office." The next time, "let's meet at the library." The next time, "let's meet at the gas station…"

When someone pictures you and remembers you, they are remembering you as this person in this place and that's all you have. Friends go places together. This is just another psychological tactic to supplant in their mind that you are a friend, you go places together. The change in scenery may also change the dynamic or level of the relationship to boost your interaction.

I cannot tell you how many times in the police world we have a "person of interest" in our custody and the interview is going nowhere. We are talking to our bad guy and we are interviewing and interviewing, nothing, nothing, nothing. Many times I have said, "You know what? I'm getting hungry. Let's go to Burger King." We get in the car and head down to Burger King. They order first, I order the same thing. (People like people like themselves.) Now we are having the burger together, we are having the Coke together and in casual conversation the next thing I know he says, "let me tell you something," and he starts confessing right there in Burger King. I save my receipt, and work the rest of my magic to finish the confession and tie it up for court appropriately.

People do business and/or confess to people who they know they can trust. You are setting yourself up for this trust by pulling all of these concepts together, talking about things the other person finds positive, finding common interests, reflecting their messages and interacting with them in different environments.

Catch Their Eye:

You need to differentiate yourself from everyone else, distinguish yourself from your coworkers, and stand out in the crowd. Remember dressing for success? That is a good start. Look at the Las Vegas strip. There are signs everywhere. So what makes any of those businesses stand out amongst any of the other businesses? In what you do, what makes you stand out against your competition? How do you get someone's interests? How do you catch their eye? There are a few different ways.

What makes you better? Do you have a better product? Do you have better customer service? What is it that you do that's any better, or any different than someone in your same exact role? Everyone has a title that someone else is doing somewhere else. So why are you any different or any better than that person in your field?

Is your customer service the best? Are you making yourself available to your target customers, checking in and following up with people after you have talked with them? Do you make sure that what ever your conversation was about that it worked for them? And if it didn't, you work together to make sure that it does happen?

Are you providing an excellent experience? Think of the difference in these two car repair examples. Imagine you take your car to shop A.

They're short with you, leave their greasy handprints on the door handle and steering wheel and a week after your repair the part comes loose. How does this leave you feeling? Now, imagine you take your car to shop B. When they return your car it's washed, vacuumed, has a clean paper mat on the floor and they tell you that your tires were low, so they filled them up at no charge. How does that leave you feeling? Where are you likely to go next time?

Activity: Catch Their Eye

Make a list of all the tangible and intangible outcomes that you provide in your business or your role as employee. Circle the ones that set you apart from others.

Now, make some notes of what you know about the customer experience at your competitor's business. Make notes of what you know about your customer's experience. Try as often as you can to get real, meaningful feedback and improve your customer's experience. What can you do better to get ahead? Here is a great take-a-way. Ask yourself this question, "How can I make it more fun for people to do business with me"? Answer this and implement, and see the advantage you have over everyone else!

Catch their eye by being the expert in your field. Become the person that people seek for all things related to your field. If your job is to mowing the lawn, be the best at doing that.

For example, if there's grass on the sidewalks and you are taking the extra time to make sure it is swept off before you leave, everything is looking perfect, you're the best. Even if people come to you with questions that you don't know the answer to, or if you are not the person that can do the job, you recommend another expert or point them in the right direction and they are going to appreciate that too. They are likely to say, "Look, I went to Matt and he didn't know but he gave me information for this guy who did and that was great," and they will talk you up just for the recommendation.

A powerful *Secret Upper Hand Tactic* for catching their eye is when talking about your business, speak to a direct pressing problem that the customer has and have their internal conversation in mind. When I retired from law enforcement, I knew that I wanted to conduct these trainings for businesses because I'm an expert. I can help people. I have experience to share.

Does anyone give a crap about me? No, they care about themselves and how I can benefit them. Now, maybe my experience comes into play for some people, but people don't want to hear about me. And they don't want to hear about you. They want you to help them solve problems. You have to think about what it is that you can do to solve their pressing issues. Let's say I am going to be a corporate entertainer, so let's think about the person booking the event. What do the event coordinators care about?

They want the guests at the party to be occupied and have a good time. They need to know that I can entertain the guests in a memorable way and ensure they have a great time. They want things to be easy because they are going to have a lot of things going on, a lot of chaos so they need to know that the booking process is easy. They want to know that they can afford it. It instills confidence when I have video testimonials of other happy clients, and I back up my services with a money back guarantee.

A preview or sample is another **Secret Upper Hand Tactic** to catch their eye. Give someone a sneak peak or a sample of your business benefits and tell them what's to come. They will want to know more. A preview or sample is a very powerful tool to evoke curiosity and it doesn't have to be a product. It could be a thought, it could be a report, and it could be anything that someone in your field is interested in.

For example, a physical therapy office is looking for potential clients. They could offer a free report on the top three muscle injuries from gardening just for filling out a quick form, which then adds you to their mailing list. It takes away the "risk" for some people and converts into sales and happy customers. Here is an example that I saw first hand in coffee sales. At a large antiques show, people walking by a booth were given a very small "free" cup of coffee so they could taste how much better this coffee was than the competition's, at the same price.

Did it work? Yes, 80% of the people who sampled the coffee were so surprised at how good it was that they bought the coffee, and most had no intention on buying coffee when they walked by.

Activity: Catch their eye through a preview

What information or goods does your business have, that you could give away a free preview or sample of? What would you want to obtain in return? Make a list. Then make a plan to release three per year.

Power words catch their eye. There are certain words that people have been found to be attracted too. A person's name is a very powerful word to use. Their name builds rapport and people like hearing their name, but don't over use it. Popular words include, "brand new", "quick and easy", "how to". Look at a lot of advertisements; these businesses and people are spending a lot of money advertising to get you in their system. Every word choice is deliberate. What works for you? What works for your competitors?

A **Secret Upper Hand Tactic** like recon, is to collect examples of items that attract your attention. How many times have you ever received junk mail and threw it away before leaving the post office? But once in a while you think, "This is interesting," and you take a piece of mail home, you open it up, and then you throw it away, right?

But something about it attracted your attention and you gave it a look. I suggest you collect things that attract your attention. It could be a fake check, flashy word or, a certain offer, a different design or clever things. There are some marketing materials that I had sent to me that I thought were interesting. I actually received in the mail a real car key. It grabbed my attention. I just had to take the car key into the car dealer to see if it unlocked the door to a car that they were giving away. You never know if that will spawn an idea in the future, but it sure piqued my interest.

I call each interesting piece that you save an 'entry' in your 'swipe file'. Start a swipe file; a collection of things that caught your attention. You might not know why today but set it aside and then over the course of time look through that swipe file and see if any ideas come to mind. It could be an idea for a presentation that you have to do. It could be just a silly joke that you heard and now you have to do a presentation and that's going to be your icebreaker.

Activity: What catches your eye?

Start a swipe file. Label a folder or a box where you can collect items that catch your eye.

A final HUGE powerful **Secret Upper Hand Tactic** to catch their eye is to tell a story about how you got started in your line of work or an interesting story that happened in your line of work. I built my career on this. I did this in the first paragraph of the introduction of this book. It worked! It piqued your interest enough that you read on.

Whatever field you are in, or whatever expertise you have, tell the story of how you got started. Or tell the story of how you helped somebody in a similar situation. Telling a story is HUGE!!! Very powerful. I have seen this time and time again how a story that has an emotional connection will seal the deal and give you the upper hand!

In simple terms this was the difference between interview and interrogation. In an interview they are talking 90% of the time and you are gathering ammunition. When you switch to interrogation, you are talking 90% of the time. What are you saying? An emotionally connected story based on truth and the ammunition they provided. Then you offer them a simple choice that is easy for them to make based on the whole process (A confession for me, a sale for you). How is this any different, law enforcement vs business? You now see how easy it was for me to make the connection and be successful in business like I was in law enforcement. Not a lot of your competitors are doing this regularly. Go steal the advantage!

Activity: Catch their eye with a story.
Write the story of how you got started in your line of work. Edit the story to be brief, appropriate and engaging.

E- EMOTIONAL CONNECTION:

Emotional connection with your customer or audience is crucial for the competitive edge. People make decisions based on emotions first and then back it up with logic. This is where a lot of people miss the boat because they don't think about engaging with someone's emotions.

This is the difference between yes and no, sale vs. no sale! If you can connect with their emotions, you can help guide them down the road to make the decision that you want them to make: buying your product, or promoting you.

Back to that ethical discussion for a moment, we are all engaging with a person to have a conversation that we have forecasted is going to have a successful conclusion in our favor. We are going to persuade them to do business with us, but we are going to persuade them in an ethical way. First, we have confidence in ourselves plus we have confidence in what we do or sell. You are going to be that kind of father-figure or mother-figure, put your figurative arm around someone and guide them on the path to success based on your expertise and your understanding of their problem.

That is leadership. You are going to lead a person to get something that is truly a benefit to them. If it is not a benefit to them, do not do it.

The **Secret Upper Hand Tactic** for engaging emotion is to understand how that person you are interacting with needs to feel in order to make the decision that you hope for them to make? If you can ask yourself that question and answer that question, then you are ready to work toward engaging that emotion. Once the appropriate emotion is engaged, they will be ready to make that choice.

Persuasion is the ability to offer compelling values to other. Notice that it's their value and not yours. Persuasion is all about being able to put yourself in the position of the other person and understand exactly what he or she wants. There are a number of techniques you can use to achieve this which will be explained shortly. To persuade others, you need to maintain rapport. The closer people feel with you, the more chances you have to convince them of your idea or products. Essentially you want to show that you think like them. Remember, people like people like themselves.

Persuasion starts with understanding the other person. Start persuasion by **listening**. In essence, the more criteria you can identify in the other person, the more options you have to satisfy them.

For example, if someone has a safety-critical mentality, you can appeal to their need for safety when selling something to them. If you are selling a car to this person, you talk about the safety benefits such as the automatic break system, side airbags and reinforced doors.

Effective listening means you need to ask questions to understand the other person better before you can attempt to persuade them. As simple as this is, it is easy to see how many people don't follow this grand rule. They go on a quest to convince the other person about their ideas, their products or services without realizing what the needs of the other person is. In effect many people become another typical salesman who can only sell what they have and not what customer wants.

WHO'S BENEFITS

Always consider the following questions when dealing with others:

What are the benefits of my product/idea to the other person?

What are the risks from their perspective?

How can I make it easy for them to agree?

Structure:

The most common form of persuading others is when you have a conversation with them individually or as a group. It is ideal if you can learn a good story in this context. To design a good story for delivery to an audience, use the following guidelines:

• **Define your overall objective.** You must know your intention. If you know what you want to achieve, it is much easier to phrase your story and also spot if your listener is drifting.

• **Define your message.** Once you know what you want to achieve, you must work on your core message that will get you to your objective.

• **Cover one subject at a time.** Your core message must be concise. Avoid complex stories. Cover one idea at a time and sequence them logically for everyone to easily follow.

• **Make the story in singular.** Don't use "us", use "I". A personal story is much more moving and inspiring than one told in general or from a third person view. Even when you quote others, present that in first person.

For example, don't say, "She said she was exhausted, she couldn't do it anymore." Instead say, "She said, 'I am exhausted, I cannot do this anymore'".

• **Stay at the right level of detail.** Match your story with your audience. Too much detail and you risk overwhelming them or drift from the main message. Too little detail and you risk telling a story about something obvious and hence boring.

• **Use real facts.** Fill your story with accurate facts, dates, names, jargon and correct terminology. This has many benefits:

• Increases credibility
• Is worth remembering by the audience

- Is more convincing
- Can be more familiar and fits better into the audience's current world view.
- Can trigger audience's memory on side stories and event. This helps them to remember your story even better.

- **Make the story emotional.** A good story appeals to our emotions. We feel for the main protagonist, we care about his misery or success, we feel overwhelmed by the bad guys and want the good guys to succeed. A story full of action and emotion is bound to be more memorable than one that is pure facts and boring data.

- **Decide on the length of your story.**
- If you have a small group of 10 to 15 people deliver a story of about 4 minutes.
- If you have a large group of 20 people or more, deliver a story of about 7 minutes.

- **Take your audience to past or future.** Many don't like the present, so take them away.

- **Appeal to sense of curiosity.** A curious listener listens more attentively.

- **If you want to say you are great, tell it from a third person view.** This approach feels less arrogant, but delivers the main message. For example, "John introduced me as the best lawyer in the country, which I was a bit taken back by..."

• **Deliver the story as something you have learned.** Formulate the story in a way that shows what you learned from someone else in the story. This way you can avoid preaching others and instead deliver your message using a character in your story.

For example,
• "It wasn't until Mary explained the concept that I realized how critical this idea was to our organization..."
• "This experience thought me..."
• "Before going through this I was lost. When I emerged from this I was a new man"

• **Include human weakness in your story.** Ego, greed, love and anger come to define many of our actions. Human weakness is just part of the deal and if you include them in your story, even about yourself, it will make it more realistic. No one would blame your weakness of chasing girls when you were 22, but would help them to fully understand what you went through and why you made those critical decisions at an early part of your life.

Remember, a persuasive story must be emotional, simple and most important, have a clear outcome so that the audience knows what you want them to do or to think.

When you are talking to people, paint pictures with words. Some people are better at telling stories than others. Story telling is your best form of advertising. If you can paint pictures with words, you can bring people through the stages of features, benefits and emotions.

Story telling success all boils down to you doing the work to come up with a true, emotionally connected story, that actually happened, that demonstrates the benefit and desired outcome for your customer by painting pictures with words to purchase your product or service. And it will show them the downside if they don't.

Activity: Create an emotional connection by painting pictures with words.

How can you explain your product through a story that explains features, benefits and engages emotions? Write it down. Practice it. Refine it.

R- Retain:

The final step in the POWER Persuasion System is to retain your relationships. It is simply not enough to close the deal, you must continue to have an ongoing relationship with your client in order to retain them. Similarly, you must continue to work on and build your personal relationships.

"YOUR BUSINESS":
First you did your homework and got the client to talk with you about your business. Then you made them feel comfortable. Next you moved them with an emotional story and closed the deal. They now know, like and trust you, so how do you keep them coming back?

Do you send them an email, newsletter or gift so you are "top of mind"? Do you send direct mail with an offer they will like? Do you have an open house or a customer appreciation day? Do you offer on going support?

You need to have a system in place to keep in touch with your customers so they continue to have a relationship with you so when the need arises you are the only logical choice.

The first of these is to just deliver a quality product or service. Selling something, or offering a service that is well made, well done, has a great shelf life. All of this will extend the rapport you've built long after the deal is done. Reinforce how great of an offer you've presented immediately after the purchase has been made. Thank them for making the decision and show them that you're still here. Send a hand written thank you note, nobody is doing that these days in the electronic world we live in. You will stand out and make another emotional connection. It is even better when you include a photo if you can.

Offering significant, long-term guarantees can really add to the confidence someone has in you and your product. And, again, keep it simple... All you have to do is tell me it didn't work. Just allow them to mail a form, click a button.

Secret Upper Hand Tactic:

Ask yourself these two questions:
- How can I make it easy for my customer to do business with me?
- How can I make it fun for my customer to do business with me?

There's one more technique I want to cover before we wrap up here, and that's reciprocity. Have you ever had a situation where you've made a decision, made a purchase, and you get a little something extra from the company?

Let's say I bought printer cartridges and they arrive with a ream of paper. Maybe I bought a car and they gave me an extra chunk of miles on my warranty. Who am I going to go to the next time I have a purchase of that nature to make? That same company. Because they've given me something, and now I want to give back. They've evoked reciprocity in me.

This works for two reasons. One, you give me something I feel emotionally, psychologically in your debt. Two, I now trust you and feel like I matter to you personally. I feel of significance. So, reciprocity really works.

Leadership:

"Leaders don't create followers, they create more leaders" - Tom Peters

A successful person is a leader in their field. You must be a leader in your field. Leadership is the ability to take charge and move others to action.

When you are working with a prospect, client or customer, and have identified and analyzed their needs, it is up to you to prepare and recommend a good, workable plan or proposal that will help satisfy those needs; a plan that's right for their situation and that fits their budget.

It's not up to the customer to tell you what they want. You are the professional. They have come to you for help and advice. You have a lot more experience, knowledge and understanding of your products and services than the customer does. You know how it is that your product/ service can improve their life. It is up to you to take charge and assume responsibility for the satisfaction and solving of their problems, needs and wants.

If you approach this with the right mix of professionalism, knowledge and confidence you'll be amazed at how many people will take your advice and follow your lead.

Here are some common qualities, taught in the supervisor's academy, that leaders possess. What person can you name for each quality when you read the list? Write them down:

–Trustworthiness	–Ability to solve problems
–Loyalty	–Enthusiasm
–Good listener	–Confidence
–Honesty	–Knowledge
–Fairness	–Good Communication
–Reliability	–Decisiveness

Sound familiar? It should if you have made it this far. The POWER Persuasion System is all leadership skills combined with ethical psychological tactics to give you that **upper hand** over others. Very powerful stuff!

As I said in the beginning, I wanted you to think about somebody who inspired you, someone that you looked up to, whether it was when you are a kid, or whether you are adult now, or someone in your field. I want you to think again about who it is that you look up to and whom you thought was a leader. What qualities did they possess that you can emulate? Now, do it. I hope you see the connection between the two lists and why.

Activity: Identify Leaders: I want you to write down the names of three people who you have looked up to in your life. Next write down the qualities they possess that you admire. Now take one quality from each person and emulate that in your life. This will take work. You now have three new leadership qualities in your life. Take note of the positive change. Set achievement dates and work on one new quality at a time. Very soon you will see the fruits of your labor.

As a leader, you embrace qualities that people can look up to. You tell compelling stories and paint pictures with words to engage powerful emotions. You look out for your customer, and ensure any decision they make with you will be a good decision for them. When people come to you with problems, you turn them into solutions.

You are a true leader people can follow. When you've mastered this, you will have loyal customers for life.

Here is a story from my experience that illustrates win/win; a solution that is good for both sides; a story that pulls this all together. Early in my career, I was part of the organized labor union with the Sheriffs. Once I was promoted to management, I was no longer eligible to be a member of the union, yet I would participate in contract negotiations.

A guy that represented our union said to me, "When we go into this contract negotiation we must have a mindset that we have to beat the management to win. We are going to go in there, we are going to win, and we are going to get something." And I said, "That's the wrong attitude to have. You are beating yourself before you even go in there, because in reality you are never, ever going to beat the management. They don't have to play your game." I went into the contract negotiation saying, "How can you benefit, and how can we benefit?" and it results in an agreement that's good for everybody involved.

You get much further ahead this way, and we actually did under my leadership in this instance. We were one of the first Sheriff's Offices in New York State to get a 20-year retirement benefit through negotiation. We got 18% raises in the same year by showing the negative impact of our extremely low rate of pay at the time.

We had to present to management the benefits that were good for them and good for us.

At the end of your day, there will be instances where what you have to offer is not truly in a person's best interest, or not what they are looking for and you cannot provide what they need. You must have enough integrity to say, "I am not the best person to help you out here but maybe I can point you to someone who can". You must have that integrity to know when you will walk away and maintain a high level of professionalism.

Debriefing: What, So what, Now what?

Debriefing is a **Secret Upper Hand Tactic** that many people wouldn't expect from a tall, confident, tough guy like myself. This is something that has helped me out in my career immensely. At the end of every major activity, I debriefed. Every crime or accident scene processed, every interrogation, every case, and every promotion. You name it, I debriefed it. Sometimes with myself and sometimes with my team.

The process I use is adapted from Kolb's Experiential Learning Cycle. It starts with a concrete experience. Then moves into reflective observation, where you ask yourself, "what just happened"? Then moves into abstract conceptualization, where you ask yourself, "so what does this mean? What have I learned from this experience?". Next, active experimentation asks yourself, "now what do I do?" to make changes to your actions based on what you have learned from an experience. The experience starts the cycle over again. In short, ask, "what?", "so what?" and "now what?".

Debriefing involves reflecting honestly on what occurred and deriving what lessons you can learn from each experience. But don't stop there. The key to success is **ACTION**. Sure, they say knowledge is power. However, if you know something but you don't apply it or take action on it, what good is it? If action is the key to success, then that's what I am challenging you to do now. Go back through the book and complete each activity. Take the tools you have learned from my book, add them to your own secrets for success and turn them into your own personal powerful persuasion communication system and gain the upper hand!

EPILOGUE

WHERE DO YOU GO FROM HERE?

Congratulations for making it this far. You have now been exposed to some of the most powerful and effective techniques, concepts and ideas available for succeeding in business and life!

No matter how good these ideas are, just being exposed to them is not enough. You must also act on them and build upon what you have learned.

I made it easy for you, anyone can do it and best of all... it works!

"If you're going to be part of a team wouldn't you want to be part of the very best?" – Navy Seal

Here is your chance to be your very best and be a part of an elite group of like-minded successful people. Go to my webpage **www.MattEpiscopo.com** and click on the **"Services/Personal Development"** tab. There you can join my prestigious **Online Academy** and **One On One Coaching Program**. I take you step-by-step through a proven process that will increase your current level of success, and make you more effective personally and professionally.

Take action now and invest in yourself because it will be a crime if you don't!!!

Go to **www,MattEpiscopo.com and sign up now**. This will give you additional content, structure and discipline you need to take your success to the next level!

Now you have the tools and information... *GO FOR IT!*

Made in the USA
Monee, IL
17 January 2020